Bears for Kids

By Jeff Fair

PRESS, INC

Box 1360
Minocqua, WI 54548

For Ian and Carrie

Published by
NorthWord Press, Inc.
Box 1360
Minocqua, WI 54548

For a free catalog describing NorthWord's line of nature and
children's books and gifts, call 1-800-336-5666.

Design by Origins Design, Inc.

ISBN 1-55971-119-1 (Hardcover)

ISBN 1-55971-134-5 (Softcover)

Why do all of us like black bears so much? Perhaps it is because black bears are so much like us. Perhaps it is because black bears seem to perform miracles. All humans love miracles.

The native peoples who first lived in North America thousands of years ago saw that black bears were like people in many ways. Like people, bears could stand tall on their back legs. Bears made tracks that looked a lot like human footprints. Bears ate about the same foods. Finally, they noticed that a bear's body was put together very much like a human's. Bears and people seemed to have a lot in common.

The early people believed that bears could lead them to the meaning of life. And they wondered about the bear's many miracles. How, for example, could the bears lie down in the autumn as if dead, and then come back to life every spring?

Before we find out, let's learn a little more about bears. Black bears are very large mammals. They live only in North America. They get their name from their thick fur, which is usually black. It may sometimes, though, be brown or tan, or blond. With their large bodies and dark fur, black bears can get very hot in the summer sunshine. (Why? Because dark colors absorb more heat than light colors.) Sometimes a bear will take a swim to cool off, or lie down in a shaded, damp place.

How big can a black bear get? Females may reach 300 pounds. Males may reach 500 pounds. The biggest black bear ever weighed was over 800 pounds. Even with all these pounds, the bears can still easily outrun the fastest human.

Black bears have a very good sense of smell, and they can hear more things than humans. Once many people believed that bears were stupid, bumbling clowns with poor eyesight. But now we know that bears are quite intelligent and curious animals. Like us, they can see color. In the Great Smoky Mountains, they can even recognize Park Rangers by their green trucks and uniforms.

Black bears have always lived in the forest. That's where we find them today – everywhere in North America where forests remain. *Deciduous forests* with plenty of nuts and acorns provide the best black bear *habitat*.

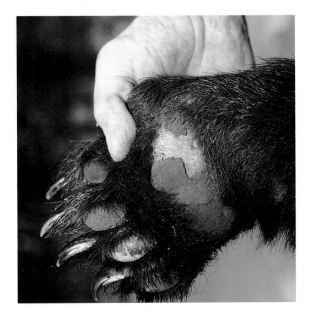

Black bears have sharp, curved claws which they use to climb trees. (The other two species of bears on this continent, brown bears and polar bears, live in more open, treeless areas and do not climb trees.) Black bears climb trees to find food, and to escape things which frighten them, which could be humans or larger bears.

Because black bears have *evolved* to climb trees to avoid danger, they rarely attack things that frighten them. This means that they almost always run away from humans. Unless they are cornered or injured, black bears like to avoid people. They are more afraid of you than you are of them.

But grizzly bears, which are one type of brown bear, sometimes attack things that threaten or surprise them. People must be more careful out West where grizzly bears live. Black bears must be more careful there, too. Grizzly bears and black bears don't always get along.

Even though black bears are not likely to try to hurt us, we must respect them. They are not pets. We should never walk up to one or try to feed one. They are wild and beautiful animals.

Dr. Lynn Rogers is a *wildlife biologist*. He has studied black bears for more than twenty years. Because black bears hardly ever attack humans, he can follow them through their natural habitat. He trusts the bears not to attack him.

In the beginning, he has to spend time with each bear to let it know he means no harm. At first, the bear is more afraid of Dr. Rogers than Dr. Rogers is of the bear. But after a long time, even a *sow* with cubs will allow him to follow closely.

Then Dr. Rogers learns about bears by spending time with them in the woods. Sometimes he spends an entire day and night with a bear family, recording everything they eat and do on his handy computer. What he records may look like this:

10:14 a.m.: *Sow eats seven bites of dandelion. Cubs are playing.*
10:17 a.m.: *Sow takes forty-two bites of grass along woods road. Cubs find blueberries—too green.*
10:22 a.m.: *Sow sits down and nurses cubs.*

Using this technique, Dr. Rogers is learning things that no scientist has ever known about black bears.

A bear that eats grasses and dandelions and blueberries? Is this all the black bear eats? Well, no, says Dr. Rogers, but it's most of what the black bear eats. The bear really isn't that good at catching other animals, even though it has sharp claws, big teeth, and powerful muscles. With a big, round body, short legs, and mild attitude, the black bear is not a very efficient *predator.*

While the black bear does eat meat when it's easy to catch, most of the animals it eats are insects: ants, bees, and yellow jackets. More than meat, the black bear eats lush new grasses, leaves, and wildflowers in spring, many kinds of berries in the summertime, and nuts and acorns in the fall.

In the fall, black bears grow fat on their feast of nuts and acorns. The layer of fat under their skin will provide them with insulation against the cold, and energy to survive the winter. A fat bear is a healthy bear.

Late in the fall, the bears begin to slow down. Their bodies are changing. Soon they will begin a long and magical sleep. We call this sleep *hibernation*.

Each bear will find its own place to hibernate through the winter. The only bears that hibernate together are mothers with their yearling cubs. Mother bears usually find a hole between rocks or under a tree in which to spend the winter. Many black bears hibernate right on top of the ground, sometimes without even the cover of a bush or low pine limb. Some bears hibernate high up in hollow trees. Bear dens average about the size of the dresser in your bedroom.

Black bears line their dens with grasses and bark and tree boughs. The dens are very hard to find. Sometimes bear dens are very close to houses, but no one (except the bears) knows that the dens are there!

Hibernation allows bears to survive the winter when none of their foods are available. In hibernation, a bear's body slows down and uses less energy. What energy it does use — just enough to stay alive — comes entirely from the fat it has stored from eating all those nuts last fall. A black bear's belly stays empty all winter. How long does your belly stay empty?

Because it lives off its fat, a hibernating bear doesn't have to get up all winter long. The bear can stay asleep in one position, without eating or producing waste, for up to six months or more! No one, not even Dr. Rogers, really knows how bears do this.

In the springtime, just as the snows are melting and the days are growing longer, black bears slowly awaken and leave their dens. It may take them two weeks or more to fully awaken and feel thirsty and hungry again. By now they may have lost one-fourth or more of their body weight. That could be as much as one hundred pounds. But their bones and muscles and eyes are all healthy, even after six solid months of not exercising them. You would look and feel terrible if you didn't exercise for six months.

Spring is the harshest time for black bears. There is little food available until the first lush grasses appear. Bears must continue to live off what is left of their stored fat. Very few black bears die during hibernation. Starvation is far more likely in the springtime.

But bears perform another miracle that no other animal can. Black bear mothers give birth to their young in January, right in the middle of hibernation. Their usual litter is two or three cubs. Litters as large as six cubs have been born to bears that live in places with lots of good food. (Fatter bears have more cubs.)

Cubs are born tiny and helpless. They look like little rats without tails. The cubs awaken frequently during winter, nurse on their sleepy mother, and grow bigger. They do not hibernate during that first winter.

Dr. Rogers often checks on the little cubs and their mothers in the early spring before they leave the den. By March, the cubs' eyes are open and their claws are already long and sharp. Holding one of them is like holding a puppy, but they sound more like human babies.

By the time they come out of their dens in the spring-time, the cubs will weigh between four and eight pounds. They will be ready to walk with mom and learn to climb trees. Knowing how to climb trees will keep them safe from many dangers.

The sow always takes good care of her cubs. She protects them and teaches them by example. When she carries her young cubs, she holds them carefully in her mouth behind her large front teeth.

These cubs will nurse through their first summer, and learn how to eat the foods their mother eats. When winter comes, they must be fat, because then they will hibernate with their mother and have no food until spring.

In the middle of their second summer, the cubs will leave their mother. Now they are on their own. Young males will wander away—often many miles away—to find their own piece of ground to call home. Young females will take a small piece of their mother's *home range* for their own. If a mother bear has a lot of daughters, she may have to move onto a new home range herself.

Young sows may have their first litters when they are between three and eight years old. Commonly, this first litter is only one or two cubs. Black bears can live to be thirty years old or more.

Few animals threaten black bears. Grizzlies can be more powerful. People are the biggest threat to black bears today. People hunt bears but also change the black bear's forest habitat.

Black bears need large areas of wooded land. They often leave an area because the forest is cut into small pieces by roads and houses and towns. Imagine how you would feel if the rooms of your house were suddenly pulled apart and separated by roads. Would you stay?

Modern people, who no longer hunt in the forest for their own food, often misunderstand wild animals like bears. At dumps and campgrounds, people often want to feed bears and pet them. (This can lead to accidental scratches, when people get way too close and then feel "attacked.") But when a bear leaves the park or the dump and comes into someone's yard, the person might suddenly feel afraid of the bear.

What we need is a better understanding of the black bear. We need to remember that bears belong in the wild. They need to be left alone.

Black bears will always be important to humans. They will continue to remind us of the wilderness, of nature's magic, and of our own past. We need to have them around us.

With a little bit of our understanding, black bears will continue to thrive.

And we should try to understand them. After all, the black bear is a wonderful animal that performs miracles!

Glossary

Here is a list of the *italicized* words in the book, followed by the page number where the word first appears and the definition of the word.

Deciduous forests: (Page 10) Forests composed primarily of trees which shed their leaves each year, such as oaks, beeches and birches.

Evolved: (Page 13) To have developed gradually (through the process of evolution).

Habitat: (Page 10) The natural environment for life and growth of an animal or plant.

Hibernation: (Page 22) Spending the winter in close quarters in a dormant or inactive condition.

Home Range: (Page 39) The area of land or habitat in which an individual animal can usually be found.

Predator: (Page 21) An animal that captures and eats other animals.

Sow: (Page 17) A female bear. (A male bear is called a boar.) Some other female animals are also called sows.

Wildlife Biologist: (Page 17) A person who studies animals.

Adult/Child Interaction Questions

How are black bears like humans?

How are they different from us?

Would you be afraid of a black bear if you saw one on a hiking trail?

Would you try to feed it?

Why do bears hibernate?

Why is it important for black bears to feast on nuts in the fall?

Why do many people feel afraid of black bears?

Should we be afraid?

Is a bear mother's care for her young in any way similar to a human mother's care for her children?

Why do you like black bears?